ISBN-13: 978-0692673270 (Hadrian Series)

ISBN-10: 069267327X

By Ina Gjikondi

Illustrated by Gianfranco Cecchetto

Foreward by Zerbanoo Gifford

Edited by Dale Lautenbach

Designed by Falguni Gokhale

Hadrian Series

First Edition

Hadrian Series Publications

www.hadrianseries.com

DEDICATION

**To our son Hadrian,
who is the Baby Light that inspires
our lives with goodness and gratitude, everyday.**

" The most beautiful experience we can
have is the mysterious. It is the
fundamental emotion that stands at the
cradle of true art and true science.
Whoever does not know it and can no
longer wonder, no longer marvel, is as
good as dead, and his eyes are dimmed. "

Albert Einstein, 1931

FOREWORD
By Zerbanoo Gifford

Ina Gjikondi's & Gianfranco Cecchetto's beautifully written and illustrated book for their son Hadrian, leaves me feeling both inspired and enlightened. This unique book makes me mindful of the magnificent source of all life LIGHT that we share wherever we live.

As a mother and grandmother I have searched for meaningful books to read with those that I adore. Books that we can enjoy and learn together about the wonders of our world. This book does that. It engages us in both the scientific as well as the spiritual knowledge that is freely available to us as is Light.

It teaches us to give time to properly observe and cherish light that surrounds us. We often forget that everyone and especially the young need to realize they are part of their environment and are influenced in the most extraordinary ways by nature that gives us such beauty in abundance. We have become so busy that we have forgotten to reflect and marvel at aspects of the world we so readily ignore or take for granted.

This fascinating book will surely become a children's classic. It brings magic back into our lives. It lightens up our everyday existence with awesome clarity and joy.

Ms. Zerbanoo Gifford is an author, human rights campaigner and founder of ASHA Centre, UK
Zerbanoo's biography " An Uncensored Life" written by Farida Master was recently launched in India and will reach the US market in 2017.

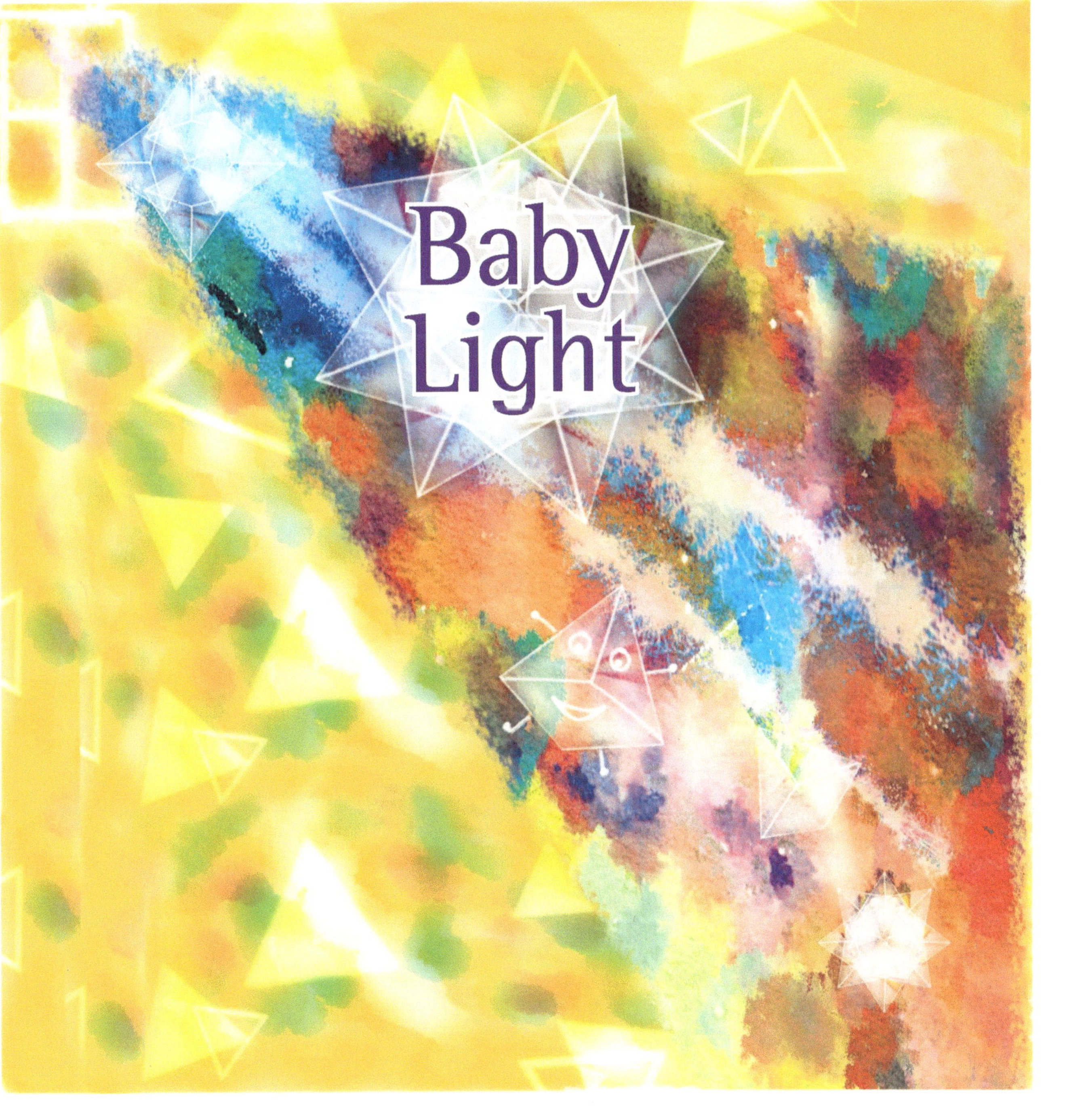
Baby
Light

It's early morning...a bright and shiny beam of light stretches warmth across your cozy bed.

Can you feel it?

Can you see it?

It wants to play with you.

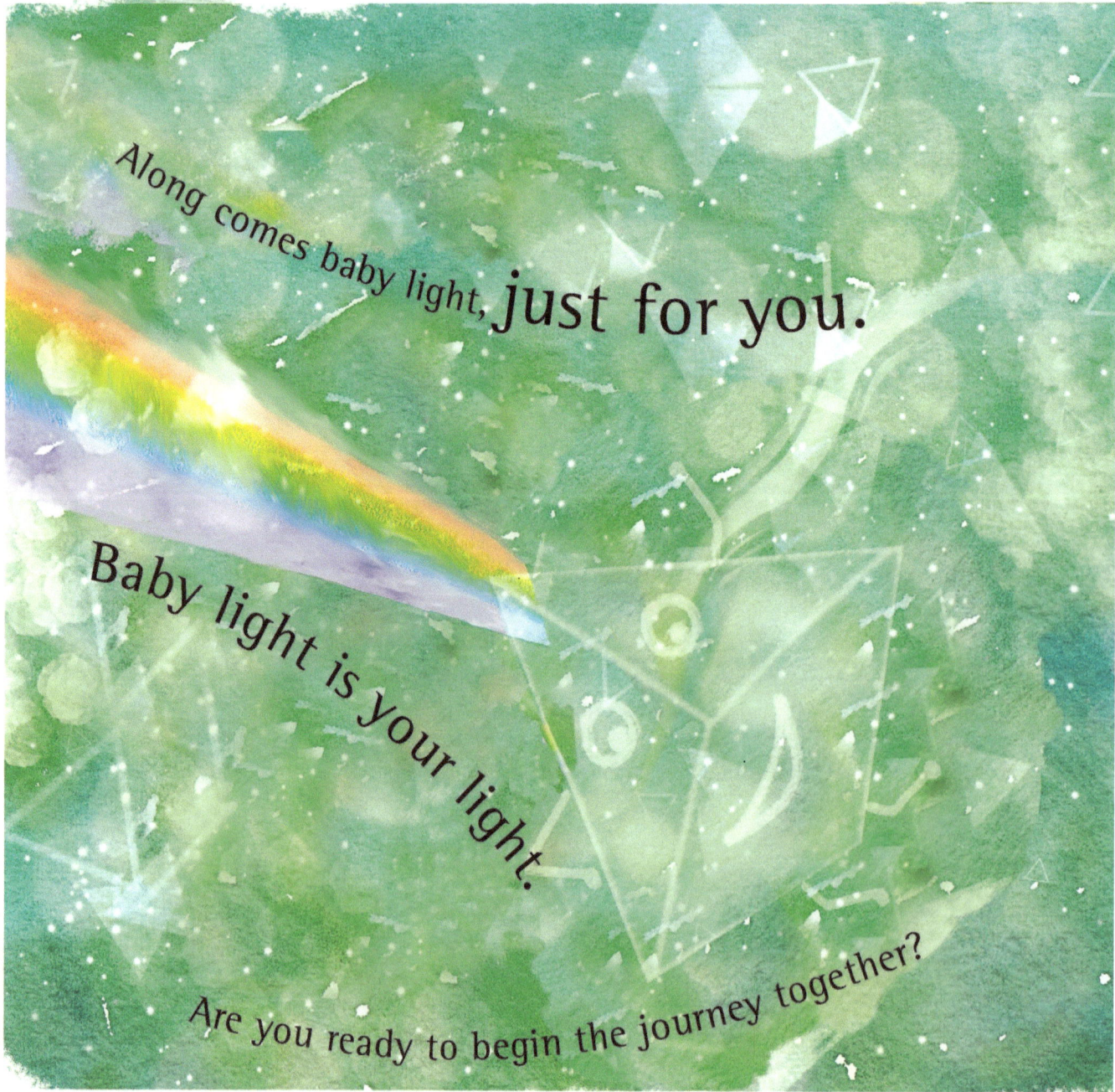

Along comes baby light, just for you.

Baby light is your light.

Are you ready to begin the journey together?

Do you want to **touch** baby light? **Hold** it in your hand?

Is that fun?

Now close your eyes again.

Can you still see the light?

Imagine you are playing with sand at the beach.

The bright sun is kissing you all over.

What does that sunlight feel like?

Is it warm like the fire,

or **cold** like the snow?

Does the light float like a feather,

or is it
heavy
like an
elephant?

Where
is the light
traveling from?

Does it come from the sun?

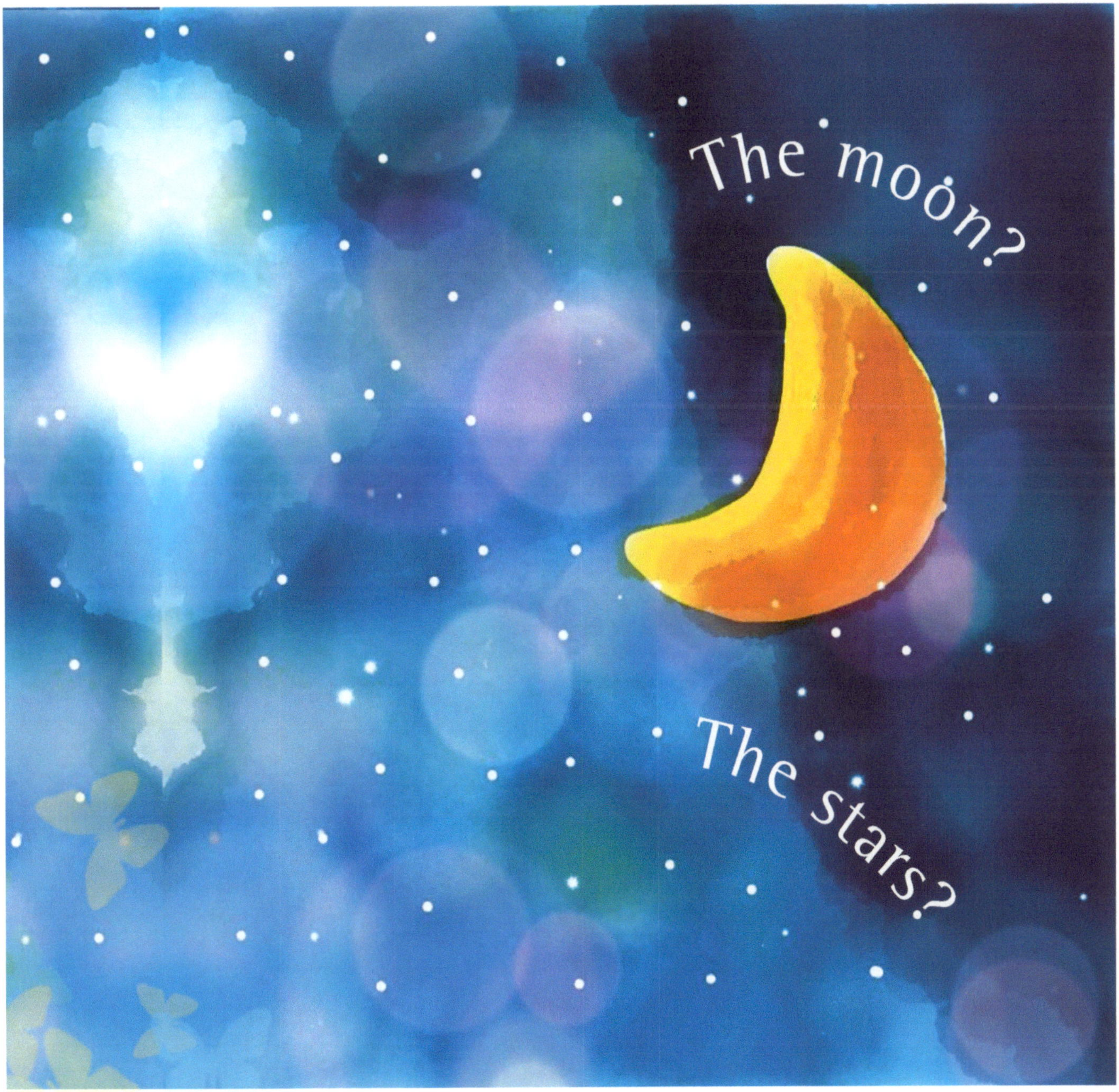
The moon?
The stars?

Is it fast like the cheetah,

Or

slow

like

a

snail?

Is the light bright like the day,

or dark like the night?

What color is the light?

Red?

Yellow?

Blue?

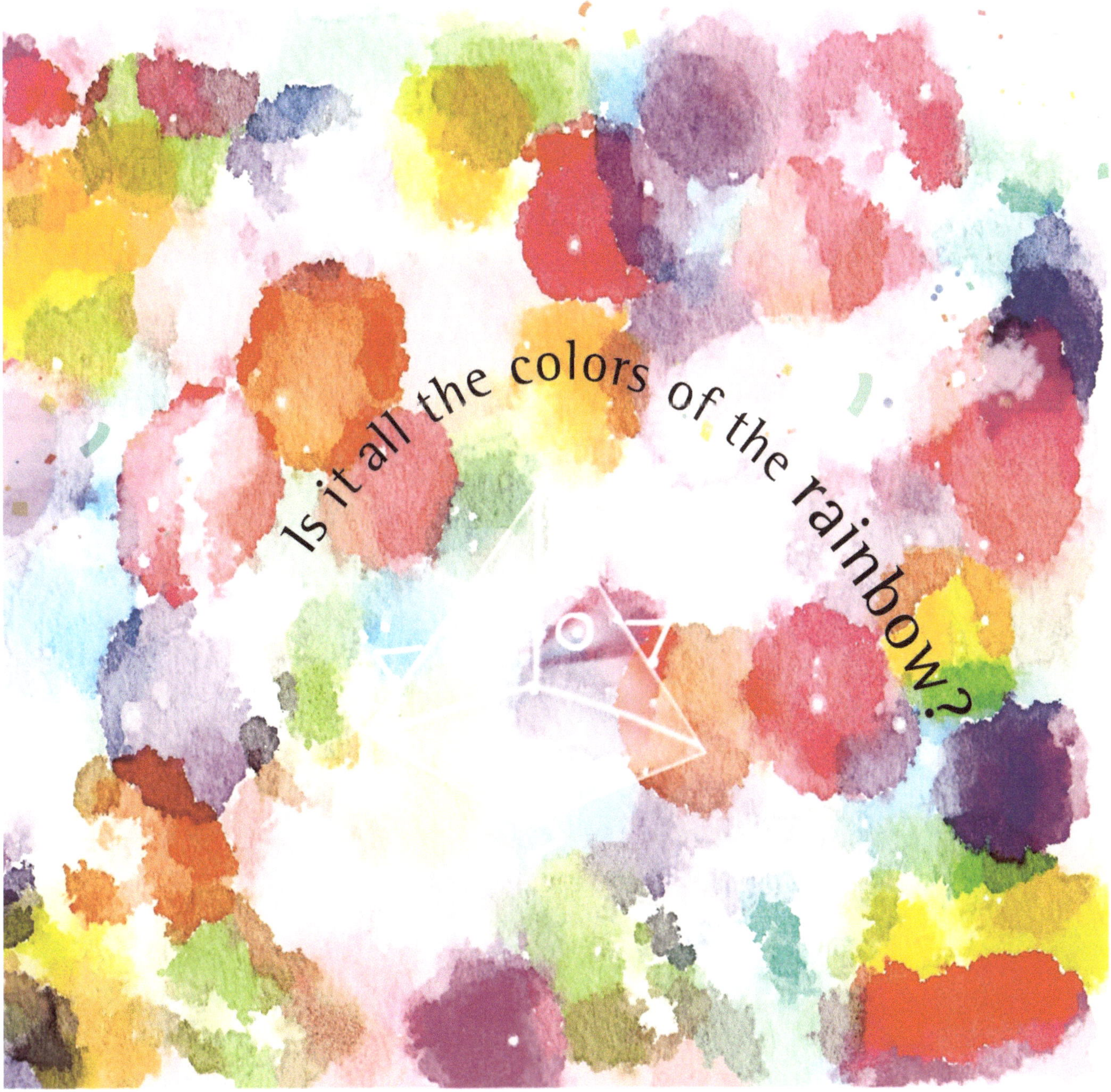
Is it all the colors of the rainbow?

Can you smell the light?

Is it sweet like a rose,

or does it smell like fresh, crisp air?

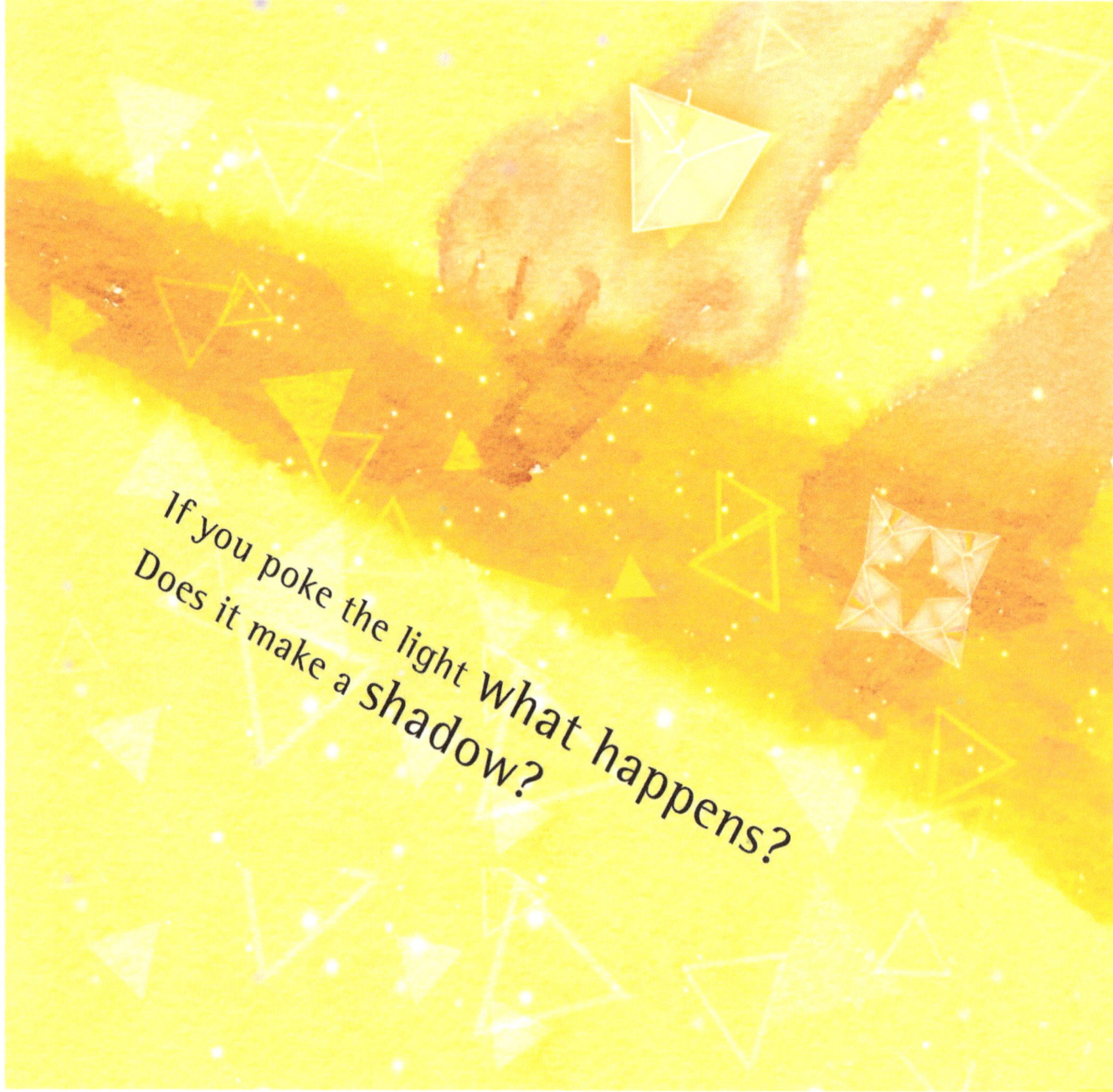

If you poke the light what happens?
Does it make a shadow?

If the light goes through the water in your glass

what happens?

What do you see?

Can you play dress-up with the light?

Wear it like a scarf?

A crown perhaps?

Try on the light. How does it feel?

Turn around and around...

Is that fun?

You look so shiny, so bright and awesome.
You look like a magic ball of yarn... and guess what,

kitty cat wants to play with you now.

You sound like a marvel.

Can you hear your song?

What's the light made of ?
Is it soft like cotton?

Or rough
like a rock?

Is the light smooth like the velvety feathers of a duck?

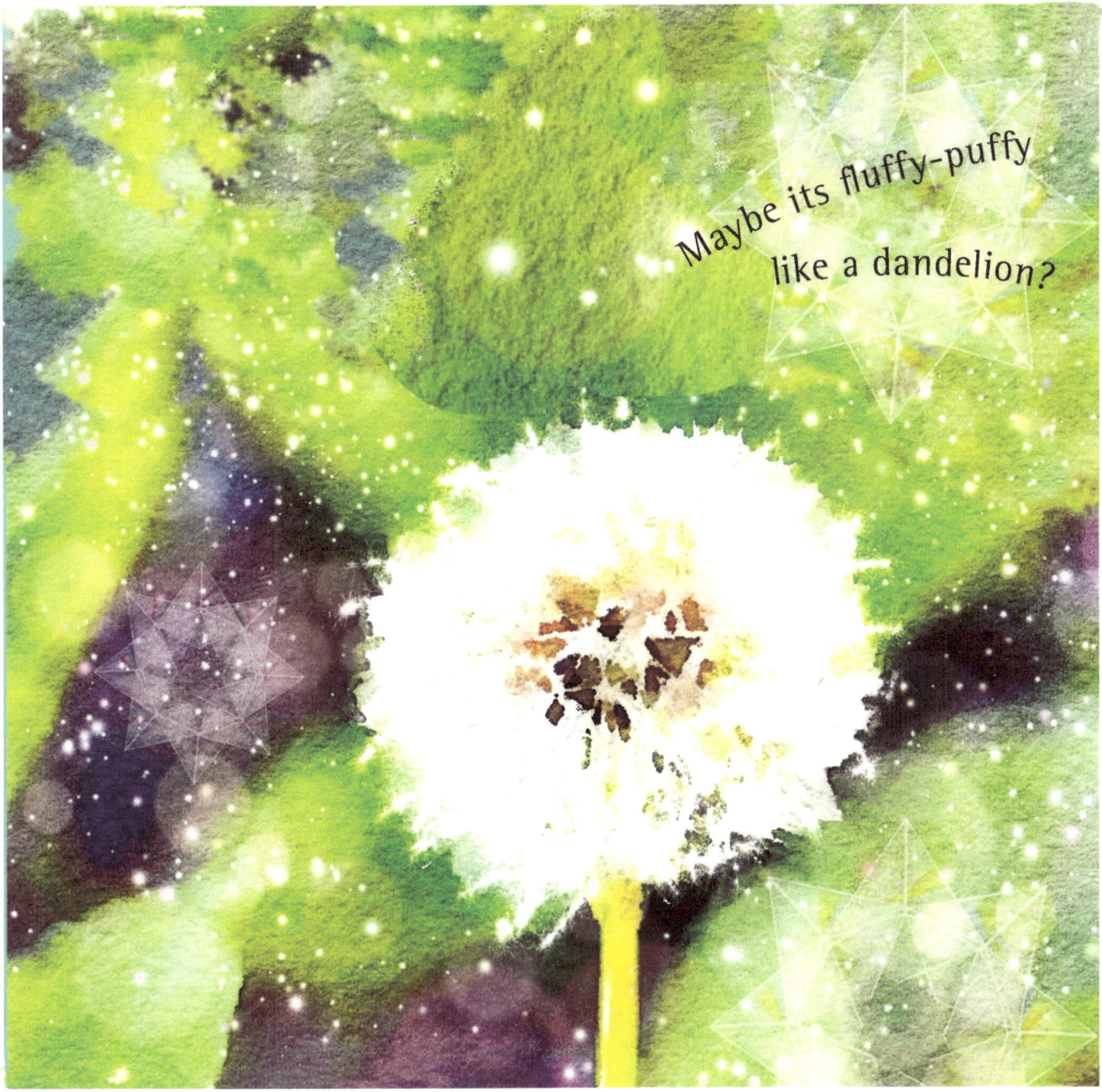
Maybe its fluffy-puffy
like a dandelion?

Does the light flow like a river?

Does it
glow
like a jellyfish?

Does it **hummmmmm** like a hummingbird?

Does it **whoosssssshhh** like the sea,

or rrrrrrumble like thunder?

What do you hear?

Now find a mirror and look closely.
What do you see?

Do you notice the glow of the light?

Can you see its
golden thread
swirling around you?

You have light all over you!

Does it feel like a big warm hug?

Now look really really close.
Can you see the tiny particles of light?

Are they like little circles?

Twinkling stars?

Sparkling triangles?

Now they are kissing your cheeks, like butterflies,

and tickling your hands, like ladybugs.

This light is in love with you.

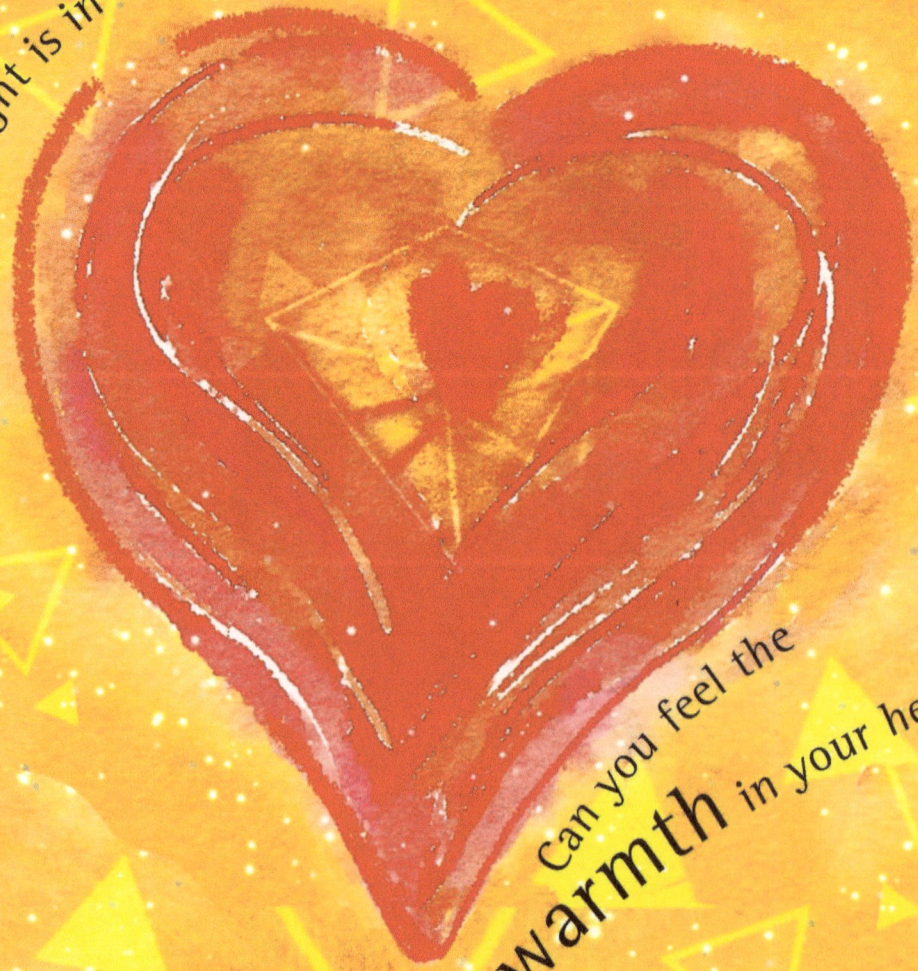

Can you feel the warmth in your heart?

Look now, the sun is setting,
the light is slowly leaving.

It will be traveling to visit other places of wonder

Let's watch it slowly melt away.

But don't be sad, the light will be back.

Let's wave goodbye,

take a deep breath in and

thank the light for this beautiful day.

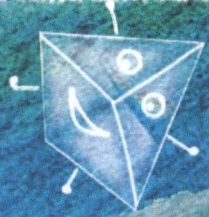

As you breathe out, the tiny particles of light swing in the air like fireflies.

They will travel the world telling your story.

You are now in the light, heart and dreams

of all the people in the universe.

Night, night
baby light!

The bright story that brought this book to life

One day, when my son Hadrian was about 1(one) and he had just started to walk, I was sitting in the living room reading, when I witnessed something extraordinary. I saw what I could have easily seen before, only that now I was "SEEING" with a new pair of eyes. I was seeing, sensing and embodying it. The sunlight had fallen inside the room and the string of light was creating quite an excitement for Hadrian, who seemed curious and playfully exploring. I saw him poking and turning around, and then going back and forth as the light appeared and disappeared in his presence. Oh, it was magical! Inside me, it felt like a stiff "Grinch" was melting down and all of a sudden I was like a child. I wanted to play and delve into wonder! It was this story that inspired the creation of Baby Light, a labor of love and passion.

I am grateful for every encounter of light, everyday.

Ina

To learn more about Baby Light and Hadrian Series please visit:
www.hadrianseries.com

FOR PARENTS, COACHES, EDUCATORS...

...and anyone who has the desire and passion to create spaces for families to come together, to learn and explore. This book supports children's growth through the art of beauty and mindfulness.

Baby Light is a story of love. It's a journey of our family coming together to play and create a new narrative. It's a celebration of the life around us, and a tribute to the sources of nourishment and inspiration that enliven our soul everyday.

Light is everywhere in the universe. It's our source of life and renewal. Baby Light offers a simple and powerful perspective in looking at what light is all about, through inquiry and playfulness. It's a way to go deeper with how beauty affects us right NOW; It's about building a mindful life, one that inspires an open mind, an open heart and an open will.

I am also compelled to see this little story be a dialogue builder, a new way of creating a space for children and parents, for families, to celebrate beauty everyday. This is an invitation and is my desire to support human beings develop emotional, cognitive, relational, somatic and spiritual competence, to serve as a foundation for growth and development and to live life to its fullest.

6 Questions you can work with to support an integral development of your child
Baby Light Book helps to observe light from a dynamic lens of inquiry, through the eyes of a child by engaging the whole being. This supports the child to build competency in 6(six) developmental streams: cognitive, relational, emotional, somatic, spiritual and integrating. (I attribute these 6 streams to New Ventures West, the coaching school that has been a great foundation for my personal development) . These six questions help explore:

1. What is light? (Cognitive)
2. What feelings does it evoke? (Emotional)
3. What happens in your body when light shows up? (Somatic)
4. What is your relationship with light? (Relational)
5. What's its impact in the universe? (Spiritual)
6. What's your story about light? (Integrating)

For an expanded list of practices and insights you may visit: www.hadrianseries.com
I would love to hear your insights and any other findings that may come up for you.

ACKNOWLEDGMENTS

It takes a family to create a book and it takes a wonderful network of friends to bring it to life.

- I am eternally grateful to my husband Gianfranco for his partnership and for helping me to see what my mind and heart was sensing.
- To Lucia and Alessandra, who poured love and joy on paper and contributed in the creation of the imagery.
- To Paolo Guerinoni, my brother in law, for offering great nature pictures that supported our creative process.
- To my sister Amantia Gjikondi, who is now taking the lead to take this book into the beautiful Albanian language.
- To my parents Rajmonda and Sazan Gjikondi, for being a great support and for taking good care of Hadrian while allowing me to work on my "passion projects".
- I am grateful to my friend Dale Lautenbach for her care, patience and for graciously reviewing and editing the book. She is not only the most amazing writer I know, but also a great source of wisdom and compassion.
- To Dr. Giovanni Dicran Megighian for his encouragement and powerful conversations that have truly supported me with my creativity. His work with MioBalance is the hidden treasure for well being.
- To Falguni Gokhale, who humbly created the design integration of this book and served as a thought partner in the process. Her ability to connect deeply and listen is a true gift.
- To Zerbanoo Gifford for being an amazing mentor and guide and for kindheartedly writing a Foreword for the book.

To my friends and coach colleagues who offered feedback and guidance:
- Joan Wangler, for her goodness and for being a strong anchor
- Betsy Caine, for her big yellow brain and for being my sounding board
- Patty Jensen, for her elegant presence and powerful language
- Julie Ellis, for her creativity and good spirits
- Anne Egseth, for guiding me into "Seeing" deeper through the Artist's Eye
- Wendy James, for looking out for me and for the genuinely good heart

I am also very grateful for my friends and colleagues at the George Washington University Center for Excellence in Public Leadership, Natalie, Jim, Kate, Samantha, Jing, Lutricia and Jiale, for their insights and just a good office life.

This book also evolved as part of my personal development work through the New Ventures West Coaching School. The richness and the depth of the program transformed my life and for that I am grateful to the faculty and my cohort colleagues.

Ina Gjikondi

How can I bring forth my goodness, beauty and gratitude in the world, NOW?

This is the question that Ina asks and allows to guide her life, in the spirit of aliveness and joy. As a mother and a human being she looks at the family as the place for creating a space of trust and play. Ina is inspired by her son Hadrian, who reminds her everyday of the gift of love and kindness. He also teaches her to slow down and to show up for life with genuine curiosity. She appreciates the diversity of human spirit, kindness, abundance, unscheduled phone calls from friends and impromptu outings, traveling, poetry, seating by the sea, music and fresh food. She continues to work on letting go of habits that no longer serve her, as she aspires to create healing spaces for people and communities, by cultivating wellbeing and empowered choice. Her place of inner peace looks like a glass dome, surrounded by water, woods and wild flowers, especially poppies, her favorites. Her desire is to continue to nurture the love for writing and publishing children, parenting and wellbeing literature. She enjoys sharing the stories that have supported her and continue to do so in life. Ina spends a good portion of her time in leadership development and coaching, as a part of the fabulous team at the George Washington University, Center for Excellence in Public Leadership. As an Albanian-American she continues to build her narrative influenced by the values of both countries and gently brings that to Hadrian with humility and care.

Ina's Mantra: "If we can just listen…. Between light and darkness there is a millisecond of stillness. I try everyday to get closer to that space, to be present for life. I am grateful for what comes as a guest into my home everyday"

Gianfranco V. Cecchetto

How might I SEE clearly in the waters that I am in?

As a passionate scuba diver, this question comes easy to Gianfranco, a wonderful father and a talented artist, in life and in the kitchen. Gianfranco has spent many years in the hospitality industry crafting beautiful meals and bringing the best out of the Italian tradition, intertwined with an elegant contemporary flavor. He is inspired by his family and his bike, which he both, did built from scratch. He loves long nature walks, water and in his wildest dreams, it's always a home by the lake that shows up. Gianfranco embodies the good quality of listening, which supports a culture of open mind and open heart.

As an Italian-American he has been the greatest teacher of the language to Hadrian and yes, a good son to his mother. Gianfranco took two years off from work, to be a stay-at-home dad and to look after his son and daughters. Gianfranco and family live in Alexandria, Virginia.

Gianfranco's Mantra: " I am a do-gooder. If I can't do this now, it's because I can't do it YET. My failures are my greatest gifts"

YOU MAY LIKE TO DRAW YOUR BABY LIGHT HERE

www.ingramcontent.com/pod-product-compliance
Lightning Source LLC
LaVergne TN
LVHW072107070426
835509LV00002B/47